The Power of Positivity

By

Natalya H. Bah, PMP, MSPM

and

Carl F. Hicks, Jr., Ph.D.

ISBN: 9781798151747

High Impact Publishing, Chevy Chase, Maryland
www.HighImpactPublishing.com

Printed in the United States of America

The Power of Positivity

Table of Contents

A Note from the Authors

Successful individuals in all walks of life often exhibit similar patterns of thinking and behaving. The authors believe it is helpful for those of you on a success journey to have the opportunity to read about and reflect upon these successful patterns of thinking and behaving that we have observed.

The authors have identified the Success Mindsets as Perspective, Purpose, and Passion and the Success Accelerators as Preparation, Positivity, and Perseverance. Each concise book in the series gives an overview of the topic identified. Additionally, each book provides questions to help you consider and increase your own level of these mindsets and accelerators.

Introduction

"Your positive action combined with positive thinking results in success."

–Shiv Khera,
Author and Activist

In our first book in the Success Mindsets and Accelerators Series, The Power of Perspective, we introduced you to Art and Dave. Art had what we described as a "balcony view" – not only literally from his second story balcony but also metaphorically as someone who never deterred no matter the obstacles in front of him. Dave, on the other hand, had a view much like the one from his basement apartment.

We described this as a confining perspective that led to frustration and his seeing only barriers not opportunities.

Art and Dave can also be looked at with the lens of positivity in addition to perspective. And our general attitude, whether it leans toward the positive or negative, can in fact impact our perspective. We can consider whether Art has a generally more positive attitude which in turn assists him in not being deterred by obstacles that present themselves. Dave may have a more negative attitude that colors those same obstacles as barriers instead of opportunities.

If you remember in the first book, Art grew and prospered which is what we find happens with people who have a positive attitude. Some may argue that we are born with a view of whether the glass is half full or half empty, but in fact, we can control how positive or negative our attitude is with self-knowledge and effort.

As you read this book, we invite you to examine and reflect on your own attitude. Take note of what kind of attitude you have throughout the day—not just externally but also in your attitude and internal dialogue with yourself. How does your positive or negative attitude impact how you work, live and succeed?

Oxford Living Dictionary defines positivity as "the practice of being or tendency to be positive or optimistic in nature."[1] What does this mean to you? How would you personally define being positive or optimistic?

1 *"Positivity." En.oxforddictionaries.com 2018. https://en.oxforddictionaries.com/ definition/positivity (24 August 2018)*

Throughout this book, we will invite you to consider and strengthen your own positivity. We have seen positivity act as an accelerator that propels successful people forward, and we want it to do the same for you.

A positive attitude creates the climate in which dreams grow, purpose and meaning thrive, goals are achieved, and you become what you believe you can be.

How does your current attitude influence how
you work, live, and interact with others?

Chapter One

Consider Your Current Attitude

"Whether you think you can, or you think you can't—
you're right."

- Henry Ford,
Founder of Ford Motor Company

If you think you can change your way of living by changing your way of thinking and you take action, then we believe you can. However, if you think that you can't change your life for the better, and you don't even try, then you won't. How we see a situation or an event or respond to people's words depends upon how we think about where we are, who we are, and what we can do. In short, how we think influences our lives and actions.

"I can do this!"

Several years ago, when one of Carl's granddaughters was about six years old, he and his wife took her to a birthday party at a bowling alley. They wondered, "How are these children going to be able to lift the bowling ball and throw it down the lane?" What they found out is that the alley adds a type of bumper to prevent gutter balls for children. If the child can toss the ball or drop it, it'll roll down the alley. With the bumper, it'll continue down the lane and most likely hit some pins.

Two children, in particular, caught Carl's attention with their different approaches to the game. The first was a three-foot tall girl who weighed about 30 pounds. Each time it was her turn, she'd become excited, jump around, and say, "I can do this. I can do this. I can do this."

She'd grab a bowling ball and struggle up to the line and drop the ball. She obviously couldn't throw it, because it was too heavy. Although she could barely make it up to the line, she'd drop the ball and then start jumping and yelling, "Strike! Strike! Strike!" The ball rolled slowly, yet it would knock some pins down due to the bumpers. Carl noticed that she actually made two strikes. It was always exciting to watch her jump up and down and just yell, "Strike! Strike! Strike!" every time she bowled.

Your *attitude* trumps your *aptitude*.

In contrast, a four-foot tall boy weighing about 15-20 pounds more than the girl would complain about the weight of the ball and how hard it was to bowl. His hunched shoulders revealed his reluctance as he walked up to the line. He was bigger and had more strength than the girl, so could put a little push behind the ball before throwing it down the alley.

After he threw the ball, I noticed he would turn to his left and walk away with his head down and a dejected look on his face. He would say, "This is too difficult. The ball is too heavy, and the pins are too far away." Almost every time, as the ball would move to the left and ride down that left bumper, it would go down and hit just one or two pins. Carl never saw him get a strike.

The young girl who was bowling with a positive attitude had what we call an internal *locus of control.*

Locus is another word for location. **People who have an internal locus of control about a certain event or activity in their life believe that they can exert some impact on the result that might occur.** Her jumping up and down and yelling, "Strike! Strike! Strike!" indicated that she believed that she could do just that, and on a couple of occasions, she actually did.

Positive thoughts ignite possibilities.
Negative thoughts limit your options.

The opposite of internal locus of control is what's referred to as an external locus of control. This refers to a belief that one can't change an outcome no matter what actions are taken and that one's results are beyond one's control.

Our loci of control varies depending upon the situation or task. For example, the very next day the boy may have had an internal locus of control when he was in art class, and the girl may have had an external locus of control when she was on the soccer field. We're always somewhere on that continuum.

Your belief system does not simply influence your future; it determines it.

Do you exhibit an internal or external locus of control most of the time?

Stop Putting Trash In Your Brain

If something is important enough to you, you'll find a way. If not, you'll find an excuse.

Sometimes we hear comments like these:

- *"I don't have enough time to get it done."*
- *"My deadlines keep me from planning more carefully."*
- *"My sales are down because I don't have good leads."*

When we hear these and similar statements, we want to ask: "Do you realize what your brain is going to do with that trash you just put into it?" We rarely do, of course.

There's a certain principle at play here, though. People who utter what we refer to as "trash" statements, are planting the seeds of an excuse in their brain. It may seem like a logical explanation, but to their brain a "permission slip" is created that looks—and very often functions—a lot like an excuse.

At best, excuses shift personal accountability and limit results. At worst, they justify failure. No one truly wants to live this way.

Before making excuses, try looking at the situation carefully, critically, and most importantly, confidently. Instead of inventing reasons as to why you can't, make plans to overcome obstacles by believing you can.

Clogging your mind with "trash" only limits your potential. Fill it with the treasure of positive thoughts and beliefs and watch the difference it makes in your life!

Chapter Two

Why Positive Thinking Matters

"Don't focus on negative things; focus on the positive, and you will flourish."

- Alex Wek,
Model and Designer

To understand why positive thinking matters, we must first understand the impact of negative thinking. This type of thinking can be described as fear, extreme concern, seeing the glass as half empty, always seeing the dark side of situations, or believing there are limited options available to us. While all of these descriptions do indeed seem "negative," research suggests that negative thinking was critical in earlier times for mankind's survival.

For example, imagine if a person encountered a wild animal while walking in the woods. Immediately, they would feel fear - which is thought to be a negative emotion. But what would be their next step? Would they write a poem, sing a song, or run away? When we're scared, our brain doesn't consider all of these options. Instead, it narrows down the options in order to help us survive. So they would obviously choose to run or fight in this instance.

Fear driven negative thinking works well in survival situations, so we can quickly select the best option. In non-survival situations, negative thinking can limit our options and possibilities and cause harm. In contrast, positive thinking expands our thinking and choices. When we feel positive, it seems more options and opportunities open up to us. This, we believe, is one of the major benefits of trying to stay in a state of positive thinking.

This brings us back to Henry Ford's remark about whether we think we can or can't, we're right. Years ago Norman Vincent Peale, in his book, *The Power of Positive Thinking*, explored related ideas to positivity by asking questions such as:

- What are some of the benefits of thinking positive?

- What's the difference between positive thinking and negative thinking?

- What does the brain do when we're thinking negatively, for instance, or what does the brain do when we're thinking positivity?

- Can we change our life in terms of our health, our goal accomplishment, the amount of money we make, even our longevity?

Now there is a whole field of study around Positive Psychology which looks at why and how people flourish and are successful. This has led to courses of study, academic research, scientific studies and more on the subject of positivity and how it impacts our lives. One expert in this field is Barbara Fredrickson, a professor at the University of North Carolina, and founder of the broaden-and-build theory. She tested the impact of positive emotions using several different research methods, including experiments with students, and she uncovered results related to the name of her theory[2].

First, she found that research subjects who were exposed to positive emotions that generated positive thinking responses tended to open up their minds to more options and to broaden their range of possibilities. Second, she found that

2 *https://en.wikipedia.org/wiki/Broaden-and-build*

their positive thinking allowed the individuals to build new skills and resources that might then provide value in other areas of their life in the future.

Positive thinking and "possibility" thinking go hand in hand.

Research shows that positive thinkers can experience increased mindfulness, sense of purpose in life, social awareness and support while experiencing fewer bouts of illness. Some studies point out that people who are positive thinkers may live longer, earn more, and have a greater group of friends. Obviously, if they're positive maybe they experience happiness and other happy people want to be around them.

The Mayo Clinic website illustrates the power of positivity by listing the following as health benefits of positive thinking:

- Increased life span

- Lower rates of depression

- Lower levels of distress

- Greater resistance to the common cold

- Better psychological and physical well-being

- Better cardiovascular health and reduced risk of death from cardiovascular disease

- Better coping skills during hardships and times of stress[3]

3 https://www.mayoclinic.org/healthy-lifestyle/stress-management/in-depth/positive-thinking/art-20043950

Can you look at your health as a measure of your positive or negative attitude?

The Fabric of Life

"Possibility, Freedom, and Choice are woven into the fabric of our lives."

-Carl F. Hicks, Jr.

Mindset is everything.

Individuals with a fixed mindset struggle with trying to envision a situation different from that which they are in. Too often they accept their circumstances, rejecting the belief that they can learn, change, or grow. In short, they settle for what they have and where they are.

Conversely, individuals with a growth mindset believe they can change their circumstances, learn different approaches, and grow to be what they were destined to be. They initiate actions to change their circumstances. They embrace the possibilities they can visualize. They recognize

their freedom to change, and they make choices that are

beneficial to them. They don't settle for the status quo.

 How about you? Do you have a fixed mindset or

a growth mindset?

 What is woven into the fabric of your life?

Chapter Three

Nurturing Your Positive Attitude

"Every day, I come in with a positive attitude,
trying to get better"

– Stefon Diggs,
American Football Wide Receiver

Play

Barbara Frederickson's research, and research inspired by her work, suggests that positive emotions build up over time with a variety of positive consequential results. So imagine how you can nurture your own positivity by ensuring you have daily experiences of positive emotions. These will then compound over time to build a wide range of resources at your disposal.

For example, she talked about the child who might be

outside running around, swinging on branches, playing with friends, and developing the ability to move from branch to branch. All of these positive emotions of joy that resulted from their playing helped the child to build skills that would be useful and valuable in everyday life.

Then maybe years later, those foundations of this athletic movement and play might lead to a college scholarship or to improved communication skills that would blossom into the possibility of success in sales. The play led to happiness that promoted the exploration and creation of new skills, even though the joy of the playing had long since ended. But the skills that were built lived on.

Play may be the opportune way to nurture and increase positive thinking in your life. Children have it scheduled into their lives. They have recess during school, after school play activities, and scheduled play dates. Adults, on the other hand, schedule time for appointments, meals, and doctor visits, but rarely schedule time for play.

**Play is relaxing and creative,
and can recharge your batteries while
also nurturing your positivity.**

Meditation

Another way we can nurture our positivity is through meditation. Jon Kabat-Zinn is a Professor of Medicine Emeritus and creator of the Center for Mindfulness in Medicine, Health Care, and Society at the University of Massachusetts Medical School. He and his colleagues have provided research evidence that meditation helps individuals "self-regulate stress, anxiety, chronic pain and various illnesses."[4]

Studies also show that meditation actually changes the brain. For instance, a group of meditation participants were asked to practice meditation daily as well as have images taken of their brain. After 27 minutes each day of meditating for just eight weeks, "participant-reported reductions in stress also were correlated with decreased gray-matter density in the amygdala, which is known to play an important role in anxiety and stress."[5]

Many successful business leaders practice meditation and some advocate it for their employees. This includes Ray Dalio, founder of Bridgewater Associates – one of the biggest

4 https://www.ncbi.nlm.nih.gov/pmc/articles/PMC3500142/

5 https://www.psychologytoday.com/us/blog/the-new-resilience/201502/how-meditation-changes-the-structure-your-brain

hedge funds in the US, Jeff Weiner, CEO of LinkedIn and Marc Benioff, founder of SalesForce.

Writing

Writing that reflects on gratitude and positive emotions can help contribute to more positive emotions as well which in turn encourages positive thinking. One method of using writing to increase positivity is through a "gratitude journal." This creates a record of what someone is grateful for on a regular basis. Studies show that there is a link between being grateful and increased well-being.

Oprah Winfrey has spoken about this type of practice and has been quoted as saying, "For years I've advocated keeping a gratitude journal, writing down five things every day that brought pleasure and gratefulness."

Through play, meditation, and writing, we can increase our positive attitude, and, in turn, increase the many benefits associated with positivity.

Positive behavior positively reinforced yields positive results.

What are five things you can think of right now that you are thankful for?

Unload That Burden

"People become attached to their burdens sometimes more than the burdens are attached to them."

*- George Bernard Shaw,
Irish Playwright, Political Activist*

Here's a potential growth exercise for you to consider: Locate either a wrist or ankle weight band (3-5 lbs) and wear it for an entire day. Put it on in the morning and remove it only after you get in bed at night.

If you try this for an entire day, you just might gain remarkable insight into other "things" that you have made a conscious decision to carry around with you. For instance, are you burdening yourself with fear, anxiety or frustration? Does carrying around one of these 'weights' every day slow you down?

Just as you can choose to strap on that wrist or ankle weight, you can choose to strap on that burden of fear, anxiety, or frustration.

And just as you can choose to unstrap that weight, you can unload those burdens that make you less than the best "you." It's your choice.

Conclusion

"Perpetual optimism is a force multiplier."

— Colin Powell
American Statesman, retired Four-Star General

What the research shows is that positive thinking really has some impact on our thinking, actions—and on the future outcome of our lives. You may wonder if positive thinking automatically leads to success and success to happiness. We would suggest you flip the order and consider whether being happy will help you become successful. We believe that if you're engaged in activities that you love to do and that you do very well and are being treated how you want to be treated, then you will most likely have a sense of positive fulfillment. You are more likely to put yourself in situations where you are engaged in the right type activities and being treated the right way if you have a positive attitude to start with.

Remember that positive thinking leads us to be more centered, focused, and open, and to have better health and live longer. The power of the mind influences our behavior. Again, how we think is everything.

Think back to the bowling alley example. The little girl who was so excited and saying, "I can do this. I can do this. I can do this" was focused on the strike and had success. The young boy who thought the ball was too heavy didn't experience the same success. Each of us need to consider what we're focused on and whether our success is being hampered by negative thoughts.

In addition to taking time to consider our own attitude and how it might be impacting our life, it's important to consider ways we can nurture having a more positive outlook. Setting aside time for play, meditation and writing can assist us in this effort. All of these can provide us with the opportunity to increase the positiveness in our life and to exploit the benefits that it can provide. Additionally, you can also develop a positively worded mantra to remind you of your efforts to nurture your positivity.

In concluding this book, we would encourage you to do additional research into the power of positive thinking. Thanks to the field of Positive Psychology, there are many resources about the topic available. And remember that positivity is an accelerator to success—and how you think will impact how fast you are propelled to success.

Reflection Questions

1. In most things that you do, do you believe that your efforts will have an impact on the results? Why or why not?

2. When you are down, depressed, stressed, upset, angry, or fearful, what happens to your mindset? Have you noticed that there seems to be a narrowing of options?

3. What techniques, methods, or processes have you acquired over your life that will help you maintain a positive thinking mindset? Is it meditation?

4. Do you keep a gratitude journal or schedule time for play in your life?

The Power of Positivity

About the Authors

Natalya H. Bah helps individuals and organizations alike define and achieve their goals. With services such as team building, executive coaching, and in-person and online training, she caters to a wide variety of interests and needs. The clients of Natalya H. Bah Consulting come from many fields ranging from legal, financial services, and real estate, to government and non-profit.

As a certified Birkman Method© consultant, Natalya utilizes the highly effective self-assessment program, along with other activities and exercises, to foster team building and strengthening in her clients. Past sessions have specifically focused on increasing effective communication, preparing for organizational change, increasing employee engagement, and understanding and meeting motivational drivers.

For her executive coaching services, Natalya created the Define and Achieve Your Goals Process™, which includes companion workbooks and online courses such as "Getting Goal Ready." This process is available for both individuals and groups.

In addition to the courses she offers online, Natalya creates and delivers in-person training on project management and leadership. She has used her training services to help organizations develop leaders, improve their project success rate, and meet their strategic goals.

Natalya has spoken at a variety of conferences and symposiums. With a relaxed, interactive facilitation style, she speaks to groups of all sizes on a wide range of topics including goal-setting and achievement, project management, self-assessments, employee engagement, and change management.

Having received her Master of Science degree in Project Management from George Washington University's School of Business, Natalya is also a certified Project Management Professional (PMP). She lives in Bethesda, Maryland, with her husband, Mahmoud, and their three children.

Carl F. Hicks, Jr., consults with successful senior executives and business owners who want more. More personal and professional growth. More productivity and profitability. More meaning and happiness. More quality thinking time.

As President/CEO of The Growth Group, LLC, Carl works with some of America's best-managed companies helping them to identify and develop their top managerial talent, strengthen their work teams, and optimize their organization's performance.

Through his conversational-coaching approach, Carl keeps clients actively engaged and focused on critical strategic initiatives, growth, and profitability - while maintaining a balance between their Life Style Goals, their Livelihood Goals, and their Quarterly Strategic Initiatives.

Clients range from emerging entrepreneurs to Fortune 100 firms. His results-oriented approach to management combines a formal education—Ph.D. in Business Administration and MBA from The University of Arkansas and B.S. in Management with Distinction from Mississippi State University — with more than thirty years of practical consulting experience.

Carl is on the Board of Directors of Lifetime Financial Growth, LLC, and has been recognized by Birkman International as a Birkman Master Certified Professional, a designation earned by only 5% of their consultants worldwide.

Carl and his wife, Carolyn, have a daughter, Natalya, and son-in-law, Mahmoud, who have blessed them with three wonderful grandchildren. Carl and Carolyn share their homes in Chevy Chase, Maryland, and Hilton Head Island, South Carolina, with Coco, their beloved Maltese.

**Also Available by Carl F. Hicks, Jr.
and
Natalya H. Bah**

The Power of Perspective

By

Carl F. Hicks, Jr.

and

Natalya H. Bah

Are you living the life you want to live? A life of purpose? Of meaning? Are you on your way to reaching the level of success you believe you're capable of? If not, it's time to harness the Power of Perspective.

Available now at Amazon.com

The Power of Purpose

By

Carl F. Hicks, Jr.

and

Natalya H. Bah

Discovering your purpose is in life is like finding the missing piece of a puzzle: all the other pieces make sense, and the meaning becomes clear. Have you harnessed the Power of Purpose?

Available now at Amazon.com

The Power of Passion

By

Carl F. Hicks, Jr.

and

Natalya H. Bah

Talent and drive are only part of the force behind achievement. The rest is passion. If you're ready to reach your next level of success, it's time to harness the Power of Passion.

Available now at Amazon.com

The Power of Preparation

By

Natalya H. Bah

and

Carl F. Hicks, Jr.

If you want to win like a champion, you must prepare like a champion. Have you harnessed the Power of Preparation?

Available now at Amazon.com

The Power of Perseverance

By

Natalya H. Bah

and

Carl F. Hicks, Jr.

Steadfastly staying the course, regardless of the setbacks and obstacles, is the only way to achieve goals and realize dreams. Have you harnessed the Power of Perseverance?

Available now at Amazon.com

Available by Carl F. Hicks, Jr.

My Growth Journal

By

Carl F. Hicks, Jr.

My Growth Journal is a compilation of inspirational quotes and challenge questions designed to encourage reflection and thought, and, most importantly . . . personal growth.

Available now at Amazon.com

The Best You

By

Carl F. Hicks, Jr.

A collection of motivational quotes by Carl to help spark a thoughtful assessment of where you are now, and inspire a vision of where you'd like to go.

Available now at Amazon.com

High Impact Ideas for Your Life

By

Carl F. Hicks, Jr.

Are you living the life you love and loving the life you live?

In this collection of thoughts and observations be inspired to rekindle your dreams, embrace your potential, and achieve what is possible in your life. Learn how to enjoy the life you were destined to live!

Available now at Amazon.com and
Barnes&Noble.com

Unlock the Growth Potential of Your Organization
By
Carl F. Hicks, Jr., Ph.D. and
Martin E. Willoughby, Jr., J.D.

With this innovative tool, learn how to understand and motivate each individual in your organization in order to achieve collective success.

Available now at Amazon.com and
Barnes&Noble.com

Are you ready for a Hicks Fix?

Visit **TheHicksFix.com** today!

Learn more about The Growth Group, LLC,
awareness and growth enhancing services:

- Executive Coaching
- Team Strengthening
- Organizational Optimization

Discover valuable resources:

- Monthly High Impact Ideas
  and Coaching Tips
- Podcasts
- Worksheets
- Videos

THE
GROWTH GROUP
Consultants to Management

Read on for excerpts from the

Power Series:

The Power of Perspective

The Power of Purpose

The Power of Passion

The Power of Preparation

The Power of Perseverance

The Power of Perspective

By

Carl F. Hicks, Jr., Ph.D.

and

Natalya H. Bah, PMP, MSPM

Excerpt

The Power of Perspective

"A change in your perspective can result in a seismic shift in your life."

–Natalya H. Bah, Co-Author

Art loved the view from his second story balcony. From that perch, he could enjoy the daily sunsets over the Pacific Ocean. He found the fading colors invigorating. His colleague Dave, on the other hand, could never see nor appreciate the sunset from his basement apartment.

Sometimes Art and Dave would have the opportunity to work together on the same project. Both were equally skilled and talented and had graduated from top universities. Yet Art and Dave's perspectives of what was possible were as different as their views from their apartments. Art had an expanding perspective and was never deterred when issues or obstacles arose. Dave, on the other hand, had a confining perspective. Dave would get frustrated by unexpected changes and saw them as barriers, not opportunities to do things better.

Art's perspective on life tended to reflect his "balcony" view. With that perspective, Art continued to grow and develop and eventually moved into his dream job. His career advancement was enhanced by his "balcony" view.

Our perspective determines how successful we'll be in our work and life. It influences how we think and see the world and how we interact with people and react to events. Successful individuals have a perspective that tends to drive them toward successful outcomes. They tend to see opportunities in problems. They look on the bright side of things and visualize results.

As you read this book, we invite you to examine and reflect upon your perspective. When was the last time that you really considered what your perspective was, and how it might be affecting your life? How does your perspective affect how you see and react to situations in your life and career? How in control of your perspective are you?

Perspective is a powerful word. It's defined by Merriam Webster as providing "the ability to understand what is important and what isn't."[1] Would you benefit from the

1. "Perspective." Merriam-Webster.com 2018.https://www.Merriam-Webster.com (7 March 2018)

opportunity to consider what is important in your life, and how you can harness this powerful tool to make you more succussful?

Throughout this book, we will provide you with questions that will help you investigate and strengthen your perspective. We hope you'll allow your perspective—hopefully from the balcony and not the basement—to drive you toward personal and professional success.

A Moment of Perspective . . .

How is your vision?

Some people view the world through the lens of rose-colored glasses. Others see the world through "woe-shaded" glasses.

But there are some who choose to wear "vision" glasses and "see" what's not there . . . but could be.

- *They see an opportunity, where others may see a problem.*
- *They see a future, where others may be stuck in the past.*
- *They envision greatness, while others experience envy or fear.*

So, how is your vision? Is it time for an eye exam?

The Power of Purpose

By

Carl F. Hicks, Jr., Ph.D.

and

Natalya H. Bah, PMP, MSPM

Excerpt

The Power of Purpose

"There are two great days in a person's life—the day we are born and the day we discover why."

–William Barclay, Author, Scholar

Knowing your *why*—your purpose—is a powerful success mindset. Typically, people can tell you what they do for a living, and how they do it, but some struggle with explaining "why" they do what they do for a living.

So, why is it important to know your "why," your purpose for doing what you do? Strong determination from the inside enhances what a person is trying to do, be, or become. A clear, internal purpose can channel your energy, provide fuel for your efforts, and keep you focused on your intentions. Once you identify your purpose, you can focus on a more intentional effort toward a goal you want to accomplish. If there's no clear purpose, you may drift off course.

Purpose transforms activity into achievement.

Purpose is defined as "the reason for which something exists or is done, made, used, etc."[1] Your reason helps you shape your vision and propels you toward your initiative or goal. When you encounter adversity, your reason helps you move forward anyway.

People who have a clear grasp of their why—and we equate that with the word "purpose"—can be truly intentional in their efforts. Your purpose comes from your values, beliefs,

1. *"Purpose." Learners Dictionary.com 2018. https://www.learnersdictionary.com*

passions, and what you determine is important to you. It comes from knowing that you have certain talents and from visualizing the results you desire. Once you have taken ownership of your purpose, no one can take it away from you.

With purpose, you can focus more on how you want to live your life—and maybe even how you want to be remembered—as opposed to only what you have accomplished. We all have purpose inside of us, but we have to nurture and shape it. You'll have to surface and enhance your purpose before it can give meaning to your life.

Do You Know Where You're Going?

Cat: "Where are you going?"

Alice: "Which way should I go?"

Cat: "That depends on where you are going?"

Alice: "I don't know."

Cat: "Then it doesn't matter which way you go."

*-Lewis Carroll, **Alice in Wonderland***

*In Lewis Carroll's classic **Alice in Wonderland**, Alice did not have a compelling "purpose" to propel her toward a desirable destination. She may eventually arrive "some place," but is it the "some place" she wanted to be? Or will she just fit herself into the "some place" she has reached?*

Some people have such a strong purpose that they are motivated to endure all kinds of hardships to reach their desired destination. Their strong purpose provides both a sense of direction and motivation to pursue a specific course of action. They will not settle for less.

Others have only a vague notion of what they want or where they are going. They become discouraged at the first obstacle. The lack of a definitive purpose provides little sense of direction and limited motivation. They will likely be tempted to settle for anything.

The Power of Passion

By

Carl F. Hicks, Jr., Ph.D.

and

Natalya H. Bah, PMP, MSPM

Excerpt

The Power of Passion

*"Working hard for something we don't care about is called stress.
Working hard for something we love is called passion"*

–Simon Sinek
Author, Motivational Speaker

Passion is a powerful force. It is the major fuel for achieving our dreams and our goals. What is your passion? When was the last time you took inventory of your passions and considered whether you are living your life pursuing them?

Passion is defined as a "strong liking or desire for or a devotion to some activity, object, or concept."[1] The more passionate we are about something, the more likely that we

1. *"Passion." Merriam-Webster.com 2018.https://www.Merriam-Webster.com (7 March 2018)*

will be successful at it. Think about people you've known who have been very passionate about their work. Doesn't it seem like those are the ones who receive the greatest notice and accolades? They live their devotion and are rewarded for it.

Sometimes we get stuck at a place in our life's journey, and we need help in getting unstuck. It may be helpful to refine, clarify, and crystalize what we are truly passionate about. We cannot overemphasize the power of passion as a propellant to helping us fulfill our dreams.

This book will walk you through rediscovering your passion by providing questions to help you think deeply about your passions. We'll then clarify your passions by revisiting activities you greatly enjoyed as a child and how to use other factors to more deeply understand your passions.

Finally, we'll discuss why pursuing your passion is

important to becoming the "you" you were meant to be.

Do I make decisions in my life without
considering my passions?

The Power of Preparation

By

Natalya H. Bah, PMP, MSPM

and

Carl F. Hicks, Jr., Ph.D.

Excerpt

The Power of Preparation

"There are other players who were more talented, but there is no one who could out-prepare me."

–Peyton Manning
Two-Time Super Bowl Champion
Five -Time National Football League Most Valuable Player

Semper Paratus –United States Coast Guard Motto

Continuous preparation is a hallmark of champions, and a strong perspective can be enhanced by intentional, purposeful, determined, definitive, and disciplined preparation. Being fully prepared occurs one step at a time, and preparation can be conceptualized as the build-up of useful skill sets over time.

Each of us needs to ask ourselves, "What skills do I need to ensure success?" and "What do I need to know how to do exceedingly well to be *Semper Paratus*—always ready?"

Intentional and purposeful preparation suggests that one devote considerable thought to the *why* and *what* of the planned preparation. Are you wanting to improve an already established skill? Do you want to strengthen a skill that has the potential for further development? The most likely response will be a "yes" to both questions.

Peyton Manning spent countless hours reviewing game film, notes by scouts, and his own thoughts in preparation for each game. He once said that he may not have been the most skilled player on the field, but he was the most prepared. A blog post by Sport Psychology Quotes (July 21, 2011) quoted Manning describing his consistent preparation:

> "In the NFL game today, there are a lot of better athletes than I am, and quarterbacks these days are faster than the quarterbacks have always been,

they're running like crazy. But I kind of stick to my roots of the disciplined quarterback. You know, I'm doing the same routine every week, studying tapes and working hard, getting ready to play and making good decisions on Sunday."

The thoroughness of Manning's preparation manifested itself in wins, MVP awards, and a number of other individual and team NFL records. In his final game as a professional football player, his team won the 2016 Super Bowl. Peyton credited his intense preparation as a contributing factor to his confidence.

Dr. Denton Cooley, the noted heart surgeon, completed the first successful heart transplant in the United States and performed more than 120,000 open heart operations during his career. He had great manual dexterity and surgical efficiency. Other surgeons commented on his lightning speed, the huge volume of daily surgeries, and his "Tiffany-level" quality. Surgeons came to Houston from all over the world to observe his procedures.

Dr. Christian Barnard said, "It was the most beautiful surgery I had ever seen. No one could equal it. Dr. Cooley's skill was matched by his grace and kindness."

His surgical procedures were focused, decisive, efficient, and effective—all outcomes of his intentional and purposeful preparation. One example of his purposeful practice involved tying knots inside of a small box as preparation for efficiently tying off surgical sutures in the confined space of a patient's chest cavity.

Champions such as Peyton Manning and Dr. Denton Cooley were able to reach the highest levels of achievement in their respective fields through dedication, hard work, and purposeful preparation. They were fortunate to have been in a calling where what they loved to do and what they did well came together.

Some may say that they were lucky. Luck may play a role, but their success did not happen by chance. Their 'luck' was the result of their preparation meeting with opportunities presented to them. "Luck is what happens when preparation meets opportunity," claimed Seneca.

The question of what to prepare for finds its response in the clarity of one's perspective. Preparation is enhanced by the clarity of your perspective. As you gain clarity about how you see the world, what you want from it, and what you are willing to do to get what you want, the preparation necessary becomes clear.

The Power of Perseverance

By

Natalya H. Bah, PMP, MSPM

and

Carl F. Hicks, Jr., Ph.D.

Excerpt

The Power of Perseverance

"On the steep slope of success can be found the victorious who are determined to persevere and to reach their dreams."

–Carl F. Hicks, Jr., Co-Author

After eighteen years of trying, Sergio Garcia won the Masters on Sunday, April 9, 2017, in his 74th attempt at winning a major golf title. He began his journey in 1999 when he first captivated golf fans at the PGA Championship. Over the years, he encountered one disappointment after another with losses and close wins. Garcia persevered through hardships and frustration and teaches us all to never give up. He's considered a true champion—not just because he won— but because he never gave up on his dream.

Success stories have three major parts: the beginning, middle, and end. In measuring success, we often focus on the difference between the start of our success journey and the completion or results achieved. The middle part, the route between start and finish, can contain ups and downs, starts and stops, and zigs and zags. It's rarely a straight line. The middle part of success can be a mixed bag.

It's in this middle part when you may start to experience obstacles. Situations can become complex and people frustrating. Sometimes, it may seem that the harder you work, the further behind you get, or you may feel trapped by circumstances beyond your control. Negative emotions can start to dominate your thinking and affect your behavior. You may entertain the idea of quitting.

It is precisely at this time that you will

need to dig deep inside of yourself and pull up all of your perseverance reserves.

I like to define perseverance as the ability to steadfastly stay the course in the pursuit of a goal, task, dream or journey, regardless of the difficulties, distractions, or obstacles faced, or the frustration and discouragement experienced. What do you think of when you hear the word perseverance? When was the last time to considered how your ability to persevere impacts your life?